AF843260

Managing and Developing Your Career as an In-house Lawyer

Authors
Ian White and Simon McCall

Managing director
Sian O'Neill

Managing and Developing Your Career as an In-house Lawyer
is published by

Globe Law and Business Ltd
3 Mylor Close
Horsell
Woking
Surrey GU21 4DD
United Kingdom
Tel: +44 20 3745 4770
www.globelawandbusiness.com

Printed and bound by Severn, Gloucester, UK

Managing and Developing Your Career as an In-house Lawyer

ISBN 9781787428515
EPUB ISBN 9781787428522
Adobe PDF ISBN 9781787428539

© 2023 Globe Law and Business Ltd except where otherwise indicated.

The right of Ian White and Simon McCall to be identified as authors of this work has been asserted by them in accordance with sections 77 and 78 of the Copyright, Designs and Patents Act 1988. All rights reserved. No part of this publication may be reproduced in any material form (including photocopying, storing in any medium by electronic means or transmitting) without the written permission of the copyright owner, except in accordance with the provisions of the Copyright, Designs and Patents Act 1988 or under terms of a licence issued by the Copyright Licensing Agency Ltd, 5th Floor, Shackleton House, 4 Battle Bridge Lane, London SE1 2HX, United Kingdom (www.cla.co.uk, email: licence@cla.co.uk). Applications for the copyright owner's written permission to reproduce any part of this publication should be addressed to the publisher.

DISCLAIMER
This publication is intended as a general guide only. The information and opinions which it contains are not intended to be a comprehensive study, or to provide legal or financial advice, and should not be treated as a substitute for legal advice concerning particular situations. Legal advice should always be sought before taking any action based on the information provided. The publishers bear no responsibility for any errors or omissions contained herein.

Table of contents

I. Introduction

1. How it all came about
In 2021 we produced a practical guide for general counsel (GC) – *Your Role as General Counsel: How to Survive and Thrive in your Role as GC* – also published by Globe Law and Business.[1] We wrote it because there was nothing we could find in the market on this subject and we would have both benefited from having a handy reference manual during our careers as GC.

The book has been well received and it occurred to us that while it was useful to have a guide for when you are at the top of your career as an in-house lawyer, the need was greater still when you were starting out and navigating through the middle ranks, or aspiring to the dizzy heights of GC. Of course, not everyone wants to be a GC – for some, being a mid-ranking lawyer is enough and there is absolutely nothing wrong with that. For others, a career as an in-house lawyer is just part of their career journey and at some point they will want to step away, taking a different direction. For others still, there are opportunities at the end of a legal career. We were keen to have a companion guide that would help all in-house lawyers – and those thinking of going in-house too – to make the best success of their career journey.

2. Who has this Special Report been written for?
While this report is primarily aimed at those considering moving in-house, away from the constraints of private practice, and perhaps

looking at a more business-oriented role – a well-thumbed title we hope will guide you on your way both day to day and over the longer term – we believe it will also be a useful reference for others such as CEOs, CFOs, HR directors and others who come into regular contact with the legal team.

3. Why you need this Special Report

One of the factors you will discover as your career progresses is that there is only one person who will really manage it, and that is you! As management guru Peter Drucker once wrote:

> *More and more people in the workforce – and most knowledge workers – will have to MANAGE THEMSELVES. They will have to place themselves where they can make the greatest contribution; they will have to develop themselves. They will have to learn to stay young and mentally alive during a fifty-year working life. They will have to learn how and when to change what they do, how to do it and when they do it.*[2]

While your organisation may, to a greater or lesser degree, help you with your career objectives and plans by sending you on relevant courses and offering on-the-job training, ultimately it will be you who is in charge of your career. In all careers, there is a certain degree of luck involved but by some careful planning you can improve your chances of having the (successful) career that you want. That may, of course, be within or outside the legal sector. It is as well that you do plan because your career is likely to be a long one, particularly if you are still in your 20s, 30s or even 40s. Drucker talked of a 50-year career, but a more recent commentator has extended this further still when talking about in-house lawyers:

> *Children aged five this year and in their first formal year of schooling, may have a seventy-five-year career to look forward to. This thought alone should make us want to question the whole idea of what a career means. It can no longer be a twenty-five-year trolley dash funnelling us along the same structured aisles of forced progression until we reach the checkout, like factory farmed middle-aged, middle-class sheep, burnt out, disillusioned and wondering what it has all been about.*[3]

This makes the planning of your career even more important – it is no longer a quick dash but more of a seasoned journey. Indeed, it is very likely that you will have many careers rather than just one. This means that you will need to apply certain skills if you are to manage your career and navigate the jobs market successfully. Drucker also identified some useful questions to ask when thinking about career planning, including:

While your organisation may, to a greater or lesser degree, help you with your career objectives and plans by sending you on relevant courses and offering on-the-job training, ultimately it will be you who is in charge of your career.

- What are my strengths?
- Where do I belong?
- What is my contribution?
- What about the second half of my career?[4]

It is worth highlighting that it is always better to concentrate on your strengths rather than your weaknesses, which flies in the face of the conventional wisdom on managing employee performance! And while you may still be at a relatively early stage of your career, it is never too soon to think about the second half. This may come sooner thank you think – later in this Special Report we look at 'portfolio careers', where you take on a number of roles simultaneously.

4. How this Special Report is set out

The first thing to say is that there are some blank "Notes and ideas" pages at the end of this Special Report. That is not because we have tried to save on the writing (!) but because we want you to be able to note your own thoughts and ideas as you work through the book. We figured that most of our readers will be lawyers, who are often precious about writing in books, but we want this to be a practical workbook where people feel they can record their thoughts and ideas as they go along. In addition, writing in the margin is not always easy.

Turning to the body of the report, we have organised the content as follows:

In chapter II we look at moving in-house – why you might want to move in-house, how you will know it is for you, how different it is and what you need to do to be successful. We also look at moving on from an in-house legal career into other functions within the business, as well as returning to private practice if that is what you want to do. We go on to look at the need to be a businessperson first and a lawyer second if you are going to truly make your mark as an in-house lawyer. This means being able to adapt to the culture of the particular organisation you are joining. Will you want to? Choosing an organisation that fits with your values and beliefs will be critically important if you are to have a successful in-house career. Finally, in this chapter, we consider when is the right time to move in-house. Is there, indeed, a right time? Does it depend on the role you are taking on?

In chapter III we consider the other functions within the business you will need to navigate. If you are armed with a Master of Business Administration degree (MBA) this may help you – and if not, an MBA may be one way of developing your business acumen. We look at the importance of strategy and leadership in business, along with functions such as marketing, operations and finance. Of course, an understanding of these is useful whether you go in-house or remain in private practice. One of the factors that will help you in your career is the need for EQ as well as IQ – and we will give attention to the important people and emotional intelligence skills as we progress.

In chapter IV we look at the skills you'll need to be an effective in-houser. These include how to manage your team, if you have one – and how to manage if you don't! – and the importance of delegating where you can. As you establish your presence you will need to start developing your team. This could, of course, include recruiting people to support you for the first time. Equally important is to retain the good people you have and motivate them to stay. As you become more senior, it is likely that you'll spend more time managing and being a trusted adviser to senior management as your knowledge of the law diminishes (yes, it's true!).

Chapter V looks at how you can develop as an effective coach and mentor, and use these skills to develop your team. What is coaching? How does it work – both within the organisation and externally? Should you train as a coach? How will it help you in your role and can you build a separate coaching career?

Chapters VI and VII look at developing your career away from the law. What options are there, whether you are in private practice or in-house? What are the type of roles lawyers transition into? And what are the (transferable) skills you will need?

In chapter VIII we look at developing your career after law and, in particular, considering the role of non-executive director (NED), bearing in mind that in this ever-changing world there is a need to reinvent yourself – regularly!

To help guide you on your way, we have included examples and quotes that provide practical guidance, drawing on the experience of a number of seasoned practitioners. We have also drawn attention to models and guidance produced by others which we believe will help you. We hope that this – and the book generally – will be of use, but only you can be the judge of that!

Finally, chapter IX contains some words of advice from people who have made a successful transition from practice to in-house.

5. A way of looking at development

At this point we think it makes good sense, both conceptually and practically, to view your professional development from a number of different perspectives, including:

- role – progressing in the role you are doing now and progressing towards the next role you aspire to; and
- skills – developing your legal skills, your business/management skills and your personal (outside work) skills and interests.

The idea is that you review both the now and the future.

In addition, it's important that you look at yourself as:

- lawyer;
- businessperson; and
- individual (ie, outside work).

Table 1 highlights what this could look like, but maybe take a moment to record your own thoughts and ideas.

Table 1: Perspectives on professional development

Role/skills	Now – in current role	Future – in potential role
Legal skills	Eg, employment law	Eg, intellectual property or M&A
Business/ management skills	Eg, team management – delegation and feedback	Eg, business strategy or legal operations
Individual/personal (outside work) skills/interests	Eg, going to yoga or helping your children to read	Eg, coaching a sports team

By looking at your development in this way you can give attention to the whole 'you'.

II. Moving in-house

1. Why? And is it for you?
The decision to move in-house – or seriously consider it – is, in itself, an important aspect of your personal development.

Therefore, it is helpful to ask some Why questions – Why move? and Why now? – and articulate the reasons. If you have spoken to friends, colleagues or a recruitment consultant you have no doubt started to do this. It will be helpful to capture your thoughts so that you can reflect on what you were thinking in the moment and see if your thinking changes over time. An incident or a particular couple of months that sparked your initial desire for a change may feel different further down the track.

A way to review your situation could be to ask the following:

- What is it that I enjoy and am good at in my current (private practice) role and what do I want to retain?
- What different types of work or work environment am I looking forward to?

The second question and your answers can get a bit theoretical and woolly. To make it much more practical, so that you can imagine it with all your senses, we suggest you walk through your perfect day in the new role. That's not to pretend that life in your new role will be perfect; but you can begin to sort out what would be essential, what would be nice to have and what does not matter so much.

Really get into the detail:

- When do you wake up and get up? Earlier or later than now?
- Where do you wake up? Where you currently live or have you moved?
- What do you wear?
- Do you travel to work or are you based from home? How much of each?
- If you travel, how do you get there – walk, car, train, bus? How long does that take?
- When you get to work, what does it look like from the outside and when you get inside?
- Are you in your own office or open plan?
- Who do you see and talk to?
- How much time do you spend at your desk – most of the time or not much?
- What sort of messages and tasks greet you?
- Are you doing mostly law or mostly management?
- Is the legal subject matter similar to what you are used to or new?
- Is it fairly narrow in scope or widely varied?
- What would you like to do at lunchtime? Quiet sandwich at your desk? Meet with colleagues? Go to the gym?
- How much of your day is with other people in meetings or online and how much on your own?
- When do you leave work?
- When do you get home?
- At home, are you doing a little/some/a lot of work?
- How are your weekends? Impacted by work or not?
- In your non-work time and holidays are you able to spend more or less time on family and personal interests?
- How will you feel at the end of the day compared with now – tired or energised?
- How will you sleep?

We appreciate that is quite a list, but which elements strike you as interesting and important? What was already on your hit list of wishes, and what might be a new consideration?

2. What makes working in-house different?

Another simple question? Perhaps, but worth delving into at the stage of deciding whether to go in-house and also as you look to progress in your in-house career.

At the most fundamental level, the biggest difference is that the purpose of the business or organisation you are joining is not to give legal advice and to be paid for doing so. We will all have been brought up to regard the law as important and difficult. It will have taken a lot of skill and hard work to qualify and make progress in a legal career. Many law firms and law firm partners rightly have powerful reputations. And the legal function in your organisation is probably (note probably) held in high regard – possibly even fear and reverence! But it will be a support function – not the core business. It almost goes without saying that you need to be clear-eyed and happy about that.

The big plus is that you can potentially create or lead a legal function that does more and does it more imaginatively and effectively than had previously been the case or been imagined. You can be someone who transforms legal from the 'business prevention department' to the 'business growth department', where your people are seen as among the brightest and best in the organisation, with whom others enjoy working.

Make a point throughout your career of seeking out and talking to successful in-house lawyers who can act as mentors – listening to you as you discuss your successes and challenges and, when appropriate,

You can be someone who transforms legal from the 'business prevention department' to the 'business growth department', where your people are seen as among the brightest and best in the organisation, with whom others enjoy working.

offering advice. The question of what makes working in-house different could be a major element of your discussions. Or you could also go down the path of working with a business coach, not an in-house lawyer, who can offer a fresh perspective. With a coach the emphasis will be on you explaining how things are and how you might want to do things differently.

3. No longer a one-way street

It may seem strange to consider this if you are now just at the stage of considering going in-house (and not so strange if you are already there), but there can be a route back from in-house to private practice. You may well be plotting your career journey one or two moves ahead and already thinking about the experience and skills you could gain in an in-house role that would benefit you, and equip you to make a significant contribution back in a law firm. That could cover either or both legal skills and management experience.

Your business sector experience could be of great value to a firm wanting to expand in that sector, in which case immersing yourself in the business issues of that sector and not just the legal issues will be vital. In some law firms they will be looking to import valuable insights and practices from the business world – a more commercial culture, better organisation, greater creativity and innovation, more accountability, better development of talented people. If it makes sense, you could look to update your CV every six months to see what experience you have gained and results you have achieved that would impress a law firm.

III. Learning about other functions – business and management skills

1. What skills are needed and where can you acquire them?
A starting point is to identify what skills are needed and where and how to get them. What do you want to learn? Of course, this is going to be very personal depending on your current role, the industry sector and your ambitions.

There are two ways to review the possibilities.

1.1 Look around your current organisation
Look around your current organisation and ask yourself and others the following questions:

- What business is it in? And/or (particularly for a not-for-profit) what is its purpose? (The ideas and writings of Peter Drucker and Charles Handy are particularly helpful in this area.)[5]
- Where has your organisation come from in terms of history and where is it going? What are its explicit strategy and stated aims? And what are the unstated priorities and ambitions? This will help you discern what skills, abilities and attitudes are going to be valuable over the next few years – which may be different to what has been important over the last few years.
- What roles and jobs do people have that are core to the business (eg, engineers in an infrastructure company, chemists

in a pharmaceutical business, coders in a software business)? What really matters to them? What do they need from the rest of the organisation in order to succeed?
- What roles and jobs do people have that support the core business (eg, you in legal, people in HR and finance)? What are the important roles and contributions that they can make? And how is that likely to change?
- What are the other divisions, departments and teams?
- How is the organisation structured? Is that changing? Is it becoming more centralised or decentralised?

1.2 Review the syllabus of a business school MBA

As we are sure our readers will be aware, an MBA is the standard post-graduate business qualification taken by people moving on and up in business. It is a path in particular for technical specialists wanting to move into a broader management/leadership role. (It's just worth pausing to reflect on how inappropriate the word 'administration' is in this context!) Of course, if formal, structured learning is not your preferred or best style of learning, then you will want to look at other options involving more emphasis on learning on the job, which is why coaching or mentoring may well be relevant and important.

One of the great advantages of an MBA programme is learning alongside people from a wide variety of backgrounds.

Topics you will typically find on an MBA programme are:

- strategy;
- finance/economics;
- marketing;
- operations;
- people/talent management;
- leadership;
- organisational design; and
- personal development.

These may not be the headings that a business school will use to describe its particular MBA programme and there will be important elements such as information management and technology that cut across these areas. In addition, most MBA programmes will offer optional modules that have a context-specific focus (eg, international business, start-up businesses or family businesses).

You can find details of MBA courses at AMBA (the Association of MBAs)[6] – the gold standard for MBA programmes in the United Kingdom – as well as international listings, for example, from the *Financial Times*.

If you look through an MBA programme, what catches your interest? What would it help you as a lawyer to know more about? If you were thinking of moving on from a legal role, what direction might that be in? One of the great advantages of an MBA programme is learning alongside people from a wide variety of backgrounds. In his MBA at Cranfield School of Management, Simon had a study group that included an engineer, a marketing executive from a paint manufacturer, a senior social worker and a submarine officer! A hugely valuable pool of work and life experience.

Turning back to those possible MBA topic headings, think about what you want or need to gain more understanding about. These may seem like very basic issues, almost too obvious. But we are great believers in the maxim that there is no such thing as a too obvious or simple question.

Typical MBA programme topics

Strategy: Does my organisation have one that I can articulate, and where would I find it? Does it give me a clear sense of the direction of the business? Who creates the strategy and how do they go about that process?

Finance/economics: How does my business generate revenue and how does it generate profits? How does it ensure adequate cash flow? How does it make and finance investment decisions. How does it raise capital?

Marketing: How does the business attract and retain customers? Reviewing the different ingredients of the marketing mix, which are most important – product, price, place, promotion, process, people?

Operations: How do the products or services of the business get created and offered to customers? What people, technology and processes need to be in place and operating effectively?

People/talent management: How do we attract, retain and develop the right people to ensure the success of the business? Are we making the most of the diverse range of talent that is available?

Organisational design: How is the business structured in order to perform to maximum capability?

Leadership: Who are our leaders and how do we identify and develop them? ('Them' on the basis that leadership is far too important to be left to one person, or even a small number of people.) What is the role of the leaders in our organisation? What behaviours do they demonstrate?

Personal development: How do I need to manage my own development for the benefit of the business and myself? (In effect, the whole subject matter of this Special Report.)

IV. Skills for the in-house lawyer

As you become more senior in an in-house role, an almost inevitable consequence is that there will be less law, and more:

- managing of people;
- involvement in business decisions; and
- being relied upon as a trusted adviser.

These are the areas where you will probably need to devote much of your personal development effort.

1. Developing your team
You may be in the position of inheriting a team or being asked to build one. In either case you will need to work back from the strategy of the business to develop a strategy for the legal function – covering in-house and external legal resources – and then to a strategy for your legal team. (We explored this process more fully in our 2021 Special Report, *Your Role as General Counsel: How to Survive and Thrive in your Role as GC*.)[7] What work does it need to be doing and what relationships need to be formed with the businesspeople across the organisation and within the team?

Different organisations will have their own versions of the post-pandemic new normal, whether people are back in the office or hybrid working. There will probably be some working practices that were functioning well pre-2020 that have been disrupted, and equally some new ways of working that will be useful going forward. Therefore, one starting point could be open conversations among the team, and with the legal team's clients, about what has changed for better or worse.

An ongoing debate will be about the size and structure of the legal team. Have we got the right number of people with the right skills and attitudes? Changes are likely to be part of an evolving process, but there may be specific moments (such as a change in the structure or strategy of the business or a significant change of budget) that create the opportunity or necessity for more radical change.

On a very practical level you will want to review how the legal team communicates, builds relationships and develops and shares knowledge. When and how does it meet – indeed, what is the purpose of people getting together? If you have six people sitting within a few yards of each other the answer may seem obvious. But it is still worth thinking through carefully, rather than assuming these issues will simply resolve themselves. If you have a hundred people in six locations around the world, then you will be looking to your HR/people managers and other business functions for ideas and guidance. A simple but effective way of developing your people is to give individuals responsibility for a particular aspect of an in-house function – for example, a region or a service/product line or an issue such as knowledge management. Delegating some responsibility and supervising such tasks will develop your own skills.

1.1 Recruitment and retention

Recruitment and retention of good people is likely to be a key part of your role as a senior in-house lawyer – and also an indicator of your success in the role. If you have not already done so, get some training and/or advice in the latest approaches to recruiting and interviewing. The younger lawyers that you may want to recruit are likely to have certain (legitimate) expectations about what a fair and enlightened process looks and feels like. An important element of this will be understanding diversity – the benefits of building a diverse team and how to make that happen.

1.2 Motivating and developing

Motivating and developing your team will be a day-to-day task, but will also be based on longer-term objectives. For example, what additional legal skills need to be developed by the team, or brought in? There are also aspects of relationships with, and management of, external law firms that you will want to improve – is that a job just for you or could other members of the team be involved? Motivation is a fascinating area in business and in life generally. It is well worth reading about, as

Fundamental to effective motivation is knowing someone – really knowing them in the sense of what makes them tick.

well as relying on your own experience and instincts. One of the key concepts in motivation is the distinction between extrinsic and intrinsic motivating factors. The former are things like pay and job titles – things that can be given to people. Intrinsic factors are those that come from within an individual, such as desire or satisfaction. It may seem obvious, but it is often overlooked that giving someone more extrinsic benefits won't resolve a need for greater intrinsic motivation. A book that we would recommend is *Drive* by Daniel H Pink,[8] an excellent mix of common sense and well-founded research. (It contains a great example of why, in the world of digital encyclopaedias, *Encarta* from Microsoft (remember that?) was a failure and *Wikipedia* is such a success.)

Fundamental to effective motivation is knowing someone – really knowing them in the sense of what makes them tick. We have worked with senior managers in the world of both law and professional football who appreciate that they cannot effectively know and motivate their people by simply seeing them in the office or on the training ground. Both have organised, say, summer barbeques in a family setting, with partners and children invited, that have opened up and strengthened mutual understanding and commitment. What could be the possible, practical options for you?

1.3 Good entrances and exits

A good test of an effectively managed and well-functioning team is how good is the process of people joining and leaving.

Joining: Have you got an established induction process? Speak to people who have joined recently to see what the experience was like for them. What worked, what didn't? What was missed out? If new people were coming to you with queries and requests, what were these about? Could it have been useful to address these at an earlier stage or was that the natural time for them to be raised? How much of the induction was about how the organisation/business works and how much about how the legal function operates? Was the balance right? Simon can remember in his first two weeks visiting the American Express call centre in Brighton and seeing the clock count down how many seconds until a customer call was answered. That was an instant and lasting reminder of what happened at the cutting edge of the business.

Leaving: Of course, there can be difficult experiences on both sides when someone leaves their job, but there is great potential for learning and continuing good relationships. The HR/people/talent team will have helpful insights on this. If, hopefully, the person is leaving happily, what feedback can they offer about their time with the organisation and how their exit has been handled? It never pays to end badly if it can be avoided. The saying, 'What goes around, comes around' is often true, as in the case of the person who leaves, goes to another in-house role and then pops up four years later as a partner in one of your key external law firms.

1.4 Delegating

As you progress, the likelihood is that you will delegate more. Think about your own experiences of being delegated to and of delegating to others. What has gone well and what has not worked? Why?

A structured delegation process

Here is a structured process for delegation that over the years has got good feedback from both people doing the delegating and those being delegated to. As you look through it you will probably see things that look obvious and you already do, and probably some new ideas.

The first thing to note is that it is a dual eight-stage process. The actual delegation briefing is the second eight-stage process and is just one element of the first eight-stage process. You may well think that 16 stages are overkill, and indeed the process should be used flexibly depending on the situation – but this very thorough step-by-step approach will be worth it when you are delegating something important, and when it really matters will give both you and the delegee peace of mind.

You will probably find that with practice the steps in the briefing process flow quite naturally and can be covered in ten minutes, although there will be times when you would want to spend an hour.

The process starts with asking yourself why you are delegating, and your approach will depend on your purpose along the following spectrum:

Getting the job done	◄———————►	**Developing the individual**
Minimising the risk		*Managing the risk*
Telling/directing style		*Asking/coaching style*

Your style of delegating should vary with your purpose in terms of risk, so that a **telling/directing style** is appropriate when you are **minimising the risk** and an **asking/coaching style** is appropriate for **managing the risk**. An obvious **starting principle** is to take time (short term) to save time (long term) so that work gets done effectively at the right level, and you can focus on more important or difficult tasks.

Eight-stage delegation process
This process potentially starts well before and finishes well after the actual delegation of work.

1. Select task
2. Select delegee
3. Prepare briefing
4. Perform briefing (see below)
5. Monitor progress
6. Liaise with other people
7. Provide feedback (NB for development situations)
8. Give opportunity for repetition (NB for development situations)

Eight-stage briefing process

This can be undertaken via a face-to-face or Zoom/Teams meeting.

1. Identify (briefly) nature of task/client
2. Check delegee's experience, commitment and availability
3. Provide context in relation to the task/client/anything else
4. Specify precise output/constraints/deadline
5. Check understanding
6. Give/invite suggestions on how to proceed
7. Agree monitoring procedure
8. Delegee to summarise and clarify initial steps

1.5 Feedback

We remember – and are always happy to share – the remark of a senior lawyer:[9]

> *Yes, drafting a mezzanine finance agreement is a high-level skill for a lawyer ... But the ability to give good feedback is a far higher level and rarer skill!*

It is, we think, one of the people skills where lawyers have the most capacity to learn and improve.

You will have your own experience of giving and receiving feedback. Once again, take some time to reflect on that experience.

Try and think of specific examples of giving and receiving feedback:

- ***Giving feedback:*** *When has someone asked you for feedback? In our experience this could be rarely, but try to remember when it has happened. When have you felt that someone needed or would benefit from feedback?*
  When have you felt confident and positive about giving someone feedback? When have you felt nervous and held back? What has been your mood and communication style when giving feedback? Have you given feedback mainly in a formal setting (eg, an appraisal meeting) or more informally and frequently? When has your feedback really helped someone to perform more effectively? When has it been rejected or not made a difference?

- ***Receiving feedback:*** *Have you invited someone to give you feedback? Have you mainly received feedback in a formal setting or as part of everyday working life? What style and content of feedback have you welcomed and appreciated? What have you resented? What has made a helpful difference?* Giving feedback effectively is a combination of a large dollop of common sense and an application of sound process. The starting point, however, is intent – the purpose and motivation of the person giving feedback. Which is why the questions above included, "What was your mood when giving feedback?" and "What style of feedback have you welcomed?".

We suggest that the intent – the motivation – has to be that you want to enable the other person to perform more effectively in the future. Perhaps obvious, yes. But think about the other possible intentions and motivations that may have been at play when you have been given feedback – or possibly when you have been giving feedback. Anger, annoyance, the desire to give someone a good telling off? We are all human and of course we experience those feelings sometimes and they can erupt spontaneously. But they are unlikely to be helpful in the context of longer-term constructive feedback. Therefore, always check your intent before embarking on a feedback conversation. It is why there may be times that you will need a two-stage process:

- Stage 1: outburst/annoyance; and
- Stage 2 (later): constructive feedback.

Tied in with this issue of intent is the idea that feedback should be for volunteers rather than conscripts. People should be welcoming rather than dreading getting feedback. (If that sounds a little idealistic, then just wait a few more lines to where we talk about a different type of feedback.)

Here is a simple four-step framework for giving feedback that in our experience people find practical and helpful:

- **Headline:** Make clear what the topic and purpose of the feedback is. For example, "I'd like to give you some feedback about that new franchise agreement you have been drafting" or, "Thinking about the meeting we had with the marketing people yesterday, could I give you some feedback about working with them going forward?". The simple purpose is that the person receiving feedback knows up front what it is about and is not left confused and guessing. (We recall lawyers from other cultures saying that British people, when attempting to give feedback, would preface it with so much talk about the weather, or what had been on TV over the weekend, or a lot of vague

Feedback can and should be used to give praise and recognition for good performance. If people start to get more familiar with feedback in the context of praise rather than criticism, then they are more likely to welcome it generally.

generalities, that the recipient would end up thinking, "What the hell was that all about!?".)

- **Replay:** Describe and explain what it was that the person did or said in some detail. For example, "The termination clauses in the franchise agreement as you have drafted them look too long and too complicated" or, "When the marketing people were getting enthusiastic about their new initiatives you were very quick in saying, 'That's just not possible'". This is in contrast to a vague and generic observation such as, "Your drafting could be clearer" or, "You need to have a better relationship with the marketing people".
- **Result/consequence:** Explain the problem (or see below ...) caused by what they have done or said. For example, "That termination clause is likely to lead to a lot of negotiating time when we are probably going to have to concede" or, "We don't want to give the impression that we are the 'business prevention department' which may mean that in future they won't want to get us involved".
- **Prescription:** Providing/suggesting an alternative, better approach. The purpose is for the person to walk away from the feedback conversation with a clear sense of what to do going forward. For example, "Let's check on the two or three serious issues where we know it has been vital to terminate the agreement in the past" or, "Let the marketing guys explain what they want and engage with their enthusiasm and say we want to help them as much as we can".

And now two very important glosses on feedback and this process.

First, regarding the "or see below" comment in the **Result/consequence** stage above, feedback can and should be used to give praise and recognition for good performance. If people start to get more familiar with feedback in the context of praise rather than criticism, then they are more likely to welcome it generally.

Of course, we are all likely to say, "Thanks, that's great!" when someone does something well. However, the more savvy (maybe more assertive) person could respond with, "Well thanks, but what was actually great about what I did – could you explain a bit more?". So, in the examples in the **Replay** stage above, feedback could have been along the lines of, "I liked the way you honed in on the practical reasons we might want to terminate, rather than just chucking in every possibility" or, "You really listened and engaged with the marketing guys". And at the **Prescription** stage you could simply say, "Do more of that!" or perhaps, "Next time we get the legal team together I want you to share that with them".

Secondly, the process as described above is – or may come across to you or the person getting the feedback as – somewhat directive, somewhat one-way, in the sense of you giving out information and instruction and the other person passively receiving it. As coaches, we have an inevitable bias towards a coaching style in business conversations, so we recommend a coaching style of feedback when possible. This means encouraging more conversation and input from the person receiving feedback. It is not a 'softer' option than just telling them, because in fact it puts more of the onus on the person to come up with their own insights and solutions.

A coaching approach to the conversations above, using the same stages, could be along the following lines:

- **Replay:** "That franchise agreement you have been working on – tell me about how you approached the termination section" or, "Thinking about the meeting with the marketing people, what happened there?". There's a subtle (or maybe not so subtle) difference between asking, "What happened?" and asking, "How do you think the drafting on the termination section went?" or, "How do you think the meeting with the marketing people went?". The quite understandable reply to those questions might be, "Er, fine I think". Then the person may feel put on the defensive if in fact what happened was less than fine. The purpose at this stage is to replay – to get them to talk through what happened/what they did, rather than to categorise it as good or bad.
- **Result/consequence:** Given time to reflect and respond and not being put on the back foot, the person may reply, "Well I tried to put in all the reasons for termination that I could think of – but maybe that's not necessary" or, "I think it went fairly well, but they were obviously not happy that I told them up front that their ideas wouldn't work – maybe I could have given them a bit more time to explain and also shown that we wanted to be helpful if at all possible". It is likely to be more helpful if the person receiving the feedback thinks things through for themselves. Which leads us to ...
- **Prescription:** The recipient may well come up with the prescription themselves. A prescription that they have generated is likely to have more impact than one they have been spoon-fed.

Does the coaching style of feedback – giving someone the time to reflect on what happened and the consequences, and then formulate their own prescription – take a little longer? Probably. But it is worth it if we go back to that fundamental idea of intent.

'Last resort' feedback

By way of postscript, there is a type of feedback that we would describe as 'last resort' and is of a different character to the developmental approach looked at above. It would be appropriate when someone has done something that is seriously, verging on dangerously, wrong. An example might be someone giving an unauthorised legally binding undertaking or instructing external solicitors who have not been accredited, without your or other appropriate authority. In that case the purpose in the first instance is to give the clear message that what has happened is wrong – and to make sure that the message has been received and accepted. A second, later, stage would be to clarify what should have been done and what should happen in the future.

The four-stage process above – Headline, Replay, Result/consequence, Prescription – is still appropriate for last resort feedback, but the prescription element may need to follow on later (and we are suggesting later the same day or the next day, not weeks later). It may be necessary to employ a broken record technique to emphasise your message – for example, "Only authorised external lawyers can be instructed by you or anyone else in the team" – and if you are met by a series of well-intended reasons/excuses such as, "But it was an emergency" or, "But I thought I should use my initiative", your response will continue to be, "Only authorised external lawyers, etc". It may be rather painful, but you want to get to the stage where the other person says, "Ok, ok, I get it!", or words to that effect. Then it will be appropriate to move on to the prescription step.

To finish this section on a brighter note: in circumstances where you are aiming to give developmental feedback, provided you genuinely feel that your intent is to help someone perform more effectively in the future, then just about anything you say or do will be of benefit to that other person.

1.6 Listening

We looked at the art and skill of listening in our earlier Special Report[10] in the context of what you will need to do during your first hundred days in a new in-house role. We do not apologise for revisiting it here briefly in the context of personal development and skills that can be improved.

Of course you want to hear compliments around the organisation to the effect that legal are great at explaining things. But is there an opportunity to hear more people say more often that legal are great listeners, they give us the chance to explain things to them, and it's clear that they really understand us?

The best starting point for being good at listening, we believe, is to take notice of people that you know are good listeners. What do they do and what do they not do? Notice what impact their good listening has on the person doing the talking. Ask them what they do – and be prepared for them to respond, "I don't know really". Persist, and probably they will be able to explain.

We like the simple mnemonic EARS as a blueprint for effective listening.

- **Empathy:** showing that you are listening through body language, gestures and simple encouragement.
- **Ask:** asking questions that you could only sensibly ask if you have been listening carefully.
- **Recap:** recapping/summarising what they have said, particularly if they have made multiple points and it would be easy for you to be a bit muddled. They can tell you if you have got it right.
- **Silence:** keeping quiet is a great way to do good listening!

In particular, look out amongst your team for the good listeners and give them feedback on what you notice them doing. That may well make you more aware of their skills.

1.7 Being a trusted adviser

Moving into the position of being a trusted adviser around the organisation, and particularly with the board, will be the ambition of most in-house lawyers who want to progress to the GC role. The concept of a trusted adviser covers a variety of attributes, but is usually understood as being in contrast to – and a significant step above – a technically competent lawyer. It is someone people will want to consult and listen to beyond when there is a legal problem to fix.

We have three general suggestions:

- A good place to start, as we have often said, is to look and learn. Who are the people you know that do this well? Not just among the lawyers but across the organisation, find those who have generated trust and credibility perhaps above their formal level of seniority. Observe them and talk to them. Spend time listening to them and understanding them. What did it take for them to move from IT specialist or finance guru to trusted adviser?
- If you want to read about this area, we recommend the always interesting and influential David H Maister *et al* and their book titled (unsurprisingly) *The Trusted Advisor*.[11] An updated 20th anniversary edition was published in 2021. The key ideas that run through Maister's books and consulting experience are

passion, principles and people – that we need to be driven by values and that relationships between people are fundamental. His view would be that yes, we want to be part of and contribute to a successful and profitable business, but that the route to that is through passion, principles and people rather than a narrow focus on success and profits.

- Finally, be or become a trusted adviser in your day job as a lawyer. Be technically competent, of course, and also know the boundaries of your expertise and when to say you don't know but can find out. Pay close attention to how legal advice is delivered by you and your team. Find how well it is understood and acted upon. Get feedback from your clients and colleagues across the organisation. We think the traffic light system is a simple way to do this – you can ask:
  - **Red:** What would you like us to stop doing?
  - **Amber:** What are we doing that would be better if changed in some way?
  - **Green:** What are we not doing that it would be helpful to start doing?

Once people know they can trust you as a lawyer and that you are open to listening to other people's views and receiving feedback, it is likely that they will value your opinions on a wider range of issues.

If you want to be a successful trusted adviser, you should be aware of the lawyer traits that you need to abandon, or use sparingly.

Hopefully they will actively ask you for them. But you may need to start by asking permission to offer ideas. You would be sensitive to someone from logistics suddenly expounding on a tricky legal problem!

This discussion about being a trusted adviser, of being more than a lawyer, reminds us of the question put by the much-respected managing partner of a highly rated international law firm to a group of current or would-be managing partners: "What do you think is the greatest impediment to you being successful in your role as managing partner?"[12]

The question produced a lot of gazing at the ceiling, head-scratching and knowing looks amongst the group. It generated answers such as, "The egos of my fellow partners – the 'herding cats' problem", "Pressure of time with so many issues to address" and, "Wanting to maintain my client relationships and skills as a practising lawyer". All valid and understandable.

His response: "It will be your training and mindset as a lawyer. The instinct to look for problems, to avoid risk, to focus on detail, to be a perfectionist."

There may have been a few more comments of that kind that you can imagine. And equally, some in the group will have thought that they were not this stereotypical lawyer; that they were creative and imaginative, looked for the positive and saw the big picture. The point being that if you want to be a successful trusted adviser, you should be aware of the lawyer traits that you need to abandon, or use sparingly.

2. Moving upwards

If you are part of a legal team that is large enough, then when you are thinking about personal development you may well be thinking about promotion.

Find out early on what is different about the more senior role that you are aiming for. You can discover this by observation if you are working closely with someone in that position. What are the technical legal skills that are required? If you are basically a real estate specialist will you need to acquire commercial law skills – or vice versa? What are the other personal or business skills that may be needed? Think back to the section earlier on business and management skills. Challenge yourself by reflecting on whether you have the skills required or can acquire them. Also ask the simple question – do you think you would enjoy the new role?

In well-structured legal departments there may well be a formal competency framework that sets out the expectations for skills and performance at different levels across a range of attributes. You may know what these are for your current role via an appraisal process, but see if you can find out what they are for the more senior role. Your GC or the HR people should have this. It makes sense to know this a year or two ahead of time and not just before you apply for a promotion. Then you can say (and have the evidence to back it up) that you have (at least to some extent) been performing at that level already.

Also find out what the process is for being promoted to a new role. Is it simply an application and an interview or is there a more rigorous process such as a development centre including role-plays or other types of tests where you need to perform to a certain standard? You may need to get, or the organisation may possibly offer, coaching or other support to help you perform to your best. This would be similar to the situation in many of the major law firms that offer coaching to lawyers applying for partnership when they have to, for example, make a business case, give a presentation, have an interview and/or take part in a selection day to test the range of competencies required of a partner.

Another element of your promotion due diligence should be to explore who will be making promotion decisions. Is it just your current, immediate report within the legal team or is it a wider group of people? If the latter, then try to do some useful networking to build up relationships.

And finally, a word for the quieter, more introverted among you (that's quite possibly 50%): let it be known that you are (quietly) ambitious and are looking for a promotion. Don't assume that by keeping your head down and doing a good, even excellent, job, the right people will realise you are keen to advance in your career. It may seem unfair if the louder extroverts get more attention, but the truth, the unfortunate truth, is that other extroverts may notice them more and be more impressed by them. In your own way, let the right people know about your ambitions. One thing you may well have in your favour as you network and seek to influence people is (returning to one of our favourite themes) that many introverts are better listeners than extroverts, who may prefer to hear the sound of their own voice. Use that to your advantage.

V. The lawyer as coach and mentor

1. Coaching

Coaching can be a useful tool for both you in your role as a lawyer, and for members of your team. While it is generally done on an individual basis, team coaching is now in vogue and is something you might consider within your department as a whole. Below we have explained what coaching is; when it is appropriate; and the value that can be gained from coaching. Much of what we have written comes from *The Sherwood Coaching Handbook*.[13]

1.1 What is coaching? What is its purpose?

To answer the second question first: effective coaching enables people to maximise their potential and perform to the very best of their ability. Coaching is designed to be of benefit to the individual and to the organisation in which they work. In fact, one of the building blocks of a successful coaching relationship (between individual, coach and organisation) is an agreed vision of what all the people involved want to achieve.

A typical coaching session is a one-to-one discussion over a period of one to two hours. It can be preceded by a telephone or virtual conversation to establish the purpose and/or key points that will be addressed and to see if there is any preparatory work that either the coach or individual should undertake. Afterwards there may be a follow-up telephone call to review progress. If a face-to-face meeting is impractical, a coaching session can take the form of a telephone/video conversation once the coach and individual have established a good working relationship.

Depending on the circumstances behind the decision to engage in coaching, there will be a series of meetings or, more unusually, a single, one-off session.

The role of the coach is to work with an individual so that they:

- increase their professional self-awareness in terms of their work, their role, how they currently approach it and their underlying motivation;
- identify what is going well and what is not, understand the causes and consider what would help them perform at a higher level;
- take responsibility for making any appropriate changes that will enable them to perform at that higher level – what they need to stop, start or carry on doing or do differently; and
- sustain and/or improve personal and business performance.

The style of the coach will generally be non-directive. The coach is not there as a trainer or expert adviser telling the individual what to do. So, in a coaching meeting the coach will spend a lot of time asking questions that help (and even force) the individual to think about their work and working relationships in a deeper way than they have done – or have had the opportunity to do – in the past.

In this context, what a coach needs to be good at is:

- prompting the appropriate self-reflection on the part of the individual, for instance by asking the appropriate question at the optimal moment;
- listening in an attentive and open-minded way;
- encouraging and helping the individual to develop their own goals, ideas, options and plans; and
- challenging where necessary to test assumptions, clarify thinking and, if required, hold an individual to account for what they commit to doing.

The end point of a coaching session will usually be a practical plan for specific action to which the individual commits – something concrete, not just a vague feeling of wellbeing.

It is helpful to distinguish between coaching and mentoring. When mentoring, the coach/mentor brings some sector- and/or role-specific

The end point of a coaching session will usually be a practical plan for specific action to which the individual commits – something concrete, not just a vague feeling of wellbeing.

knowledge – that is, they have been there, seen that and done it too. Of course, coaching and mentoring can overlap – with powerful results. External coaches may have particular sector or role experience that provides credibility and can be a source of useful insights. Equally, there can be an advantage in having a coach who doesn't have knowledge of your profession or sector, as the temptation to interfere and impose their own views can be a material disadvantage.

1.2 In what circumstances can coaching be of value?
Examples of where coaching pays dividends include the following:

- where someone is taking on, or aspiring to, a new role and new challenges through promotion or a change in responsibilities such as taking charge of a business group or function;
- where building and leading high-performance teams becomes a key element of an individual's job – in short, they need to be a coach to their team;
- where steering a business or organisation through significant change is the priority for someone in a leadership role;
- where there is a need for new or existing teams to work well and achieve results together; and
- where creating a learning and coaching culture is required across an organisation.

1.3 When is coaching appropriate?
Here are some specific examples:

- An established leader seeking to implement change and/or facing difficult decisions wants an independent and confidential sounding board.
- Following (or in preparing for) promotion, someone wants to understand and meet new expectations – for example, becoming a partner or board member or working in a new environment.
- There is a requirement to get to grips with a new role following a lateral career move, for example, to chief executive, head of department or senior manager. This could involve support through 'the first 100 days'.[14]
- There is a need to develop new skills, especially interpersonal skills, as a priority; for example, for running team meetings, holding important one-to-one conversations or appraisals and managing conflict. Many otherwise confident and experienced professionals can struggle when strong emotions (their own or others) surface and have to be addressed.
- A new team is created or an existing team is given a new task, and they need to explore how to work together most effectively.
- A high-performing professional is interested in exploring motivation and finding the next big challenge.
- An individual needs to prepare for a specific challenge – for example, putting together a business case, presenting to a new client, speaking at a conference or taking part in a selection day for promotion.

In each of these situations coaching offers tailored support that can accelerate the individual's (or team's) learning, effectiveness and development. The focus is on helping people raise and maintain their game.

An external coach who has some shared experience with the individual (eg, has been a partner or senior manager in a law firm or similar business) may be able to combine the benefits of coaching and mentoring but it is important to define the parameters of the coaching element if this is the case.

1.4 When is coaching not appropriate?
Coaching (at least on its own) is not appropriate where what the person really needs is:

- technical training;
- effective line management; and/or
- therapy or counselling (responsible business coaches should not

stray into areas where they are not qualified to help – though they can act as a catalyst for a client who needs this to seek appropriate support elsewhere).

Finally, effective coaching is built on the assumption (which may need testing) that the individual is a volunteer and has the physical and psychological energy to set and work towards challenging goals.

1.5 The lawyer as coach
While many people look for an external coach there is no reason not to use an internal coach, who will normally be:

- a senior manager in a leadership role, such as CEO or COO, department head or practice group leader;
- another senior manager in the business from a completely different area of work from the relevant individual, who is a naturally good coach and part of an internal coaching support network; or
- a senior support professional, such as the business development or human resources director.

Effective coaching is built on the assumption (which may need testing) that the individual is a volunteer and has the physical and psychological energy to set and work towards challenging goals.

(a) Senior managers in leadership roles
This person may be the obvious candidate to undertake a coaching role – they know the person and the circumstances. What they may lack are the skills, the inclination and, importantly, the time. Some senior managers will be able to adopt an effective coaching style and still be demanding bosses who, for example, carry out performance appraisals. Others will find it difficult to combine these approaches. In addition, exceptional sector-specific expertise can get in the way of an effective coaching relationship. The 'expert' may feel more comfortable addressing issues of technical competence, but this may be missing the point.

(b) Other senior managers
Some of the best coaches can be within the organisation but not technical experts in the same field as the person being coached. An interesting experiment was carried out in the sports world that showed there were certain circumstances in which ski coaches performed better than tennis coaches at coaching tennis![15] This was because the ski instructors were forced to focus more on listening to and understanding the person they were working with, rather than focus on the correct technique. This is the so-called 'inner game' in which the opponent in tennis, or the barrier to top performance in golf, is the voice inside one's head saying what one must – or should – do rather than the person on the other side of the net or the difficulty of the golf shot! The senior manager from another department who is not going to tell the individual how to do their job and is not going to carry out their next appraisal may get a better reception than the boss.

Using senior managers in this role will entail finding people with some natural aptitude and a willingness to learn more about coaching. Then it will be a matter of finding or creating opportunities for them to practice.

This approach can create a group of people with credibility who have a positive impact on the performance of others and at the same time perhaps break down unhealthy divisions between teams or departments. We usually find that acquiring coaching skills makes people more effective in leading and managing their own people as part of the day job as well.

(c) Business service professionals
Coaching by senior business services or support professionals (who are not formally trained coaches) can be very effective within their area of responsibility, eg, a BD director coaching on running pitches or an HR director coaching on developing better team working.

A qualified professional may prefer the opportunity of a one-to-one conversation rather than going on a traditional training programme, which may be seen as the 'remedial' option. Again, it will be a question of the business support person having the appropriate style, skills and time.

Some organisations are now investing in coaching training for their senior business services professionals and recognising that coaching is a key part of their role.

1.6 Using coaching techniques in your everyday work

There is no reason why you can't act as a coach either to members of your team or to other people within the business. You probably use coaching in your everyday work either as a manager or when you are dealing with legal issues and projects. You may not even realise you are doing so!

Coaching techniques – whether you have developed them yourself or you have seen them used by others – can be a part of your day-to-day work. There are a number of models – you can find many of them in books as such as *The Little Book of Big Coaching Models*[16] – that can be utilised. One model we particularly like, which you can adopt in meetings, for coaching or in your everyday life is Nancy Kline's 'Thinking Environment'. Her ten components of a thinking environment are very useful tools both in your role as a GC and also in how you work with your team. They are:

Attention: *Listening without interruption and with interest in where the person will go next in their thinking*

Equality: *Regarding each other as thinking peers, giving equal time to think*

Ease: *Discarding internal urgency*

Appreciation: *Noticing what is good and saying it*

Encouragement: *Giving courage to go to the unexplored edge of thinking by ceasing competition as thinkers*

Feelings: *Welcoming the release of emotion*

Information: *Absorbing all the relevant facts*

Difference: *Prioritising diversity of group identities and understanding their lived experience*

Incisive questions: *Freeing the human mind of untrue assumptions lived as true*

> ***Place:*** *Producing a physical environment – the room, the listener, your body – that says, 'You matter'*[17]

Another tool you can use is Neil's Wheel.[18] Neil's Wheel is a free tool for concerned citizens, professional coaches and clients, that can easily and consistently open up deeper, inspiring and transformative conversations. It will allow you to discuss different components of your (and your team's) life, aspirations and objectives.

2. Mentoring

As previously mentioned, it is important to recognise that mentoring is different from coaching. The mentor brings sector- and/or role-specific knowledge to the table – in relation to the individual, they have been there and done that. Remember also that coaching and mentoring can overlap, with powerful results. Paul Gilbert, of LBC Wise Counsel, defines mentoring as follows:

> *[Mentoring is] a confidential, respectful, non-judgemental conversation to explore issues and ideas of the moment as well as to help individuals develop their skills and their potential as an in-house lawyer. Most of our mentors have been senior in-house lawyers, but we also have mentors with different career/life experiences. Although there is a lot of debate about the differences between coaching and mentoring we make the distinction that coaches should be formally qualified as coaches, follow a recognised methodology and be judged against specific outcomes. Mentoring however is less formal, offering senior and experienced peer support albeit in a structured way.*[19]

You may decide to act as a 'mentor' to your team but really this is more like line management rather than true mentoring. However, there is no reason why you can't mentor someone and talk through issues they have because you too have faced them in your career, and this can be enormously valuable. Whilst having someone with a similar background as a mentor can be very helpful, it is also useful for people to have someone as a mentor who has a different background. Therefore, you could mentor a person in a different department – HR, for example. Some companies encourage mentoring from employees elsewhere in the business, and this can be very productive.

So why might someone want to use you as a mentor? Over to Paul Gilbert again – as a very experienced mentor some of the reasons he has identified for mentoring include:

- Personal career development
- Handling difficult relationship issues in the workplace
- Developing your leadership credentials

- Personal effectiveness
- Managing time and priorities
- Articulating your value
- Your next move
- Handling a career gap and returning after a break
- Moving into a non-legal role[20]

There are now also things such as 'reverse mentoring', where a more junior employee mentors a more senior one. So, you might find yourself mentoring the CEO!

VI. Developing your career away from law (but in a legal environment)

One route for your future development could be working in a legal environment but not as a lawyer. The most obvious examples of this would be taking on a role as a chief executive in a law firm or a barristers' chambers.

Your background legal knowledge will be of benefit and perhaps most importantly, from the perspective of your new colleagues, it will give you credibility. You will have come through similar qualifications, training and experience as them. Of course, going forward, having been (or even still being) a good lawyer is not what will matter or what you will be judged on.

1. What does the new organisation need from you?

Part of your research about a potential new organisation will be to look carefully at the role and what is expected of you.

The business skills discussed in chapter IV will provide an indication of what could be relevant.

Does the organisation need a new approach to or improvement in any of the following?

- strategy;

- finance/economics;
- marketing;
- operations;
- people/talent management;
- leadership;
- organisational design;
- personal development; or
- something else?

And always be on the lookout for any discrepancy between what the organisation (or at least the people you are talking to) says it wants and what, with a bit of research, you find out it really needs.

A starting point for getting a handle on the new role will be some sort of job description. However, it may be that you are the first into a newly created role and there is none available. Or the organisation may be looking for you to do something very different from the previous incumbent.

2. What will you be doing?
In any event, we would say be wary of job descriptions. A long list of detailed tasks and (frequently jargon-ridden) accountabilities is often

Always be on the lookout for any discrepancy between what the organisation (or at least the people you are talking to) says it wants and what, with a bit of research, you find out it really needs.

not a good indicator of the realities of the role. A different approach is to try to imagine for yourself and find out from the organisation what your working week would consist of – how you would actually be spending your time. You can do this by creating a week in diary format and populating it with activities. So first thing on a Monday morning what do you think you would be doing? How about late Tuesday afternoon? Thursday lunchtime? Sometime over the weekend? Of course, not every week will be the same, so you could, for example, think about one week in May and one in September if those are particularly important times of the year. In any event, find some way to compare and contrast how you and the organisation see the realities of the job.

A few indicators might include the following:

- How much time are you in the office and how much elsewhere?
- How much time are you at your desk and how much around the premises?
- How much time are you on your own, and how much in one-to-one or larger meetings?
- Is it a 9 to 5, five-days-a-week role?

An example of when this approach proved useful (in fact, vital) for us was when working with a barristers' chambers taking on their first chief executive. There was an enormous disparity in views between the barristers. Some were expecting the new person to be predominantly at their desk, at the end of a phone or screen, able to deal with their requests during the day; while others saw the job as outward-facing so that the new person would often be out with clients or at events, or meeting potential new members. (What was needed was the latter.)

The ultimate test is to match up you, the role and the organisation's expectations and to ask the simple but important questions: What does success look like? At the end of your first year (or other appropriate timeframe), what is it that you want to have achieved? And how do you want to feel about your own performance and development?

If it helps, you can use the familiar SMART objectives format:

- **S**pecific: what in detail, rather than generally, do you want to achieve?
- **M**easurable: how will you measure your achievements so that you know whether you have achieved them?
- **A**chievable: choose objectives that are realistic.
- **R**elevant: choose objectives that are aligned with your overall goals and those of the organisation.
- **T**imed: have a timetable for success.

3. Conclusion

We think that someone with senior in-house legal experience could be ideally suited to an important leadership and management role in a law firm or barristers' chambers. Go in with eyes wide open!

VII. Developing your career in-house (but not as a lawyer)

What are the options when you become GC? They include:

- serving on an executive committee;
- becoming the company secretary;
- moving from a legal role to one such as chief risk officer, compliance director, chief people officer or head of ethics and sustainability;
- leaving the law and going into the business;
- becoming CEO; and
- leaving the business.

1. Getting to be GC or a similar role

As we outlined earlier, there are less roles the more senior you become. This is natural as there can only be one ultimate boss. While some larger groups may have a GC and divisional GCs beneath this, most companies have relatively small legal teams and there will normally only be one GC. Given the number of in-house lawyers there now are, not all of them will get to become GC and so it is important to ensure you plan your career carefully if this is what you aspire to. It doesn't guarantee success, of course, but it gives you a much better chance of getting there. You can read much more about the role in our companion Special Report, *Your Role as General Counsel: How to Survive and Thrive*[21] so we won't go into detail here.

Your legal skills will be taken as a given, but it is worth briefly rehearsing some of the additional qualities that you may need for the role of GC:

- This is from the Heidrick & Struggles report, *Do you have the right C-Suite?* where it relates to GCs:
  CEOs are looking for someone who can not only act as a trusted legal adviser of impeccable integrity, but also act as a valued business partner. In addition, the GC should be able to work collaboratively with the senior executive team to achieve business goals.[22]
- While you will probably report to the CEO or CFO (and you may have a dotted reporting line to the chair) your ultimate client is the company itself and you need to ensure you remember this as well as your overriding duties as a lawyer. There is a need to manage this perceived conflict of interest – there will be times when what the CEO may want to do is not in the best interests of the company, and it may not even be legal. You will need the resilience to stand up to the CEO – who, as we have outlined, may be your boss – without fear or favour. This is not always easy in practice, but unlike with some other professions, as a lawyer you will have duties over and above those to your client.
- You are likely to work with the board much more closely as GC. This can require careful navigation and if you have not come into contact with the board before it is worth finding out as much as you can about how they work and operate in practice. If there is a separate company secretary it would be worth talking to them about this but if you have access to the chair that will give better insight still.
- And finally, remember that getting to GC is one thing, but remaining there is quite another. Being able to adapt to the (right) culture and values will be critical to your success or otherwise.

2. The options when you become GC or a senior lawyer

Well, at last you've made it – you're GC! What now?

To start with and depending upon the size of your team, you are likely to have a lot on your plate: safeguarding the organisation's legal and regulatory position; probably managing a team although some GCs work alone; working with various colleagues; perhaps working with the board; acting as a trusted adviser to the senior team; and attending lots of meetings ... The list goes on. So, it is unlikely that you will be short of work.

Remember that getting to GC is one thing, but remaining there is quite another. Being able to adapt to the (right) culture and values will be critical to your success or otherwise.

Becoming GC may mean that you also have to take on a wider role within the organisation – one that isn't solely legal – for example, either serving as an adviser to the executive committee or being a member of that body. Or it could mean taking on a completely new role such as company secretary, which you might combine with that of GC or take on separately, depending on the size of the roles and the support available to you. You could also transition into other roles such as chief risk officer, chief people officer or head of ethics and sustainability. Going down these routes may enable you to look at even more senior roles leading up to CEO. And, finally, you may eventually decide to leave business altogether!

The following sections look at these various possibilities.

2.1 Acting as an adviser to/being a member of the executive committee

As GC you may well either have to act as an adviser to – or sit on – the executive committee, or 'exco'. The exco is made up of the principal heads of the business and support functions. It normally comprises the CEO, CFO, chief people officer, divisional managing directors and, depending on the sector, roles such as chief risk officer and head of compliance. The purpose of the exco is to run the business – it is the operational leadership team that reports into the board. Excos can take two main forms: a CEO exco which advises the CEO, who in turn acts as a decision maker alone, and a full exco which makes decisions and recommendations to the board as a group. Both are still headed by the CEO.

Some companies have the GC as a full member; in others he or she may be an attendee. Sometimes the GC does not attend exco unless there is a specific legal issue that has come up that needs their advice. Where you will sit as a GC will depend on the organisation concerned, but if you are going to be a full member you really need to bring more to the party than just your legal expertise, particularly if you sit on a full, rather than just a CEO, exco. That said, it is important to remember that you are primarily there for your legal expertise: we recall one GC being very frustrated that the CEO wouldn't listen to him on matters of strategy even though there was a perfectly able strategy director present. You wouldn't want the marketing director advising on legal matters – or at least we hope you wouldn't – so it is important to stick to your (legal) brief and opine on other matters only when needed.

There is a long-running debate as to whether the GC should sit on the exco at all. A rough estimate would suggest that in about 50% of cases the GC is a member of the exco, and this is an increase on ten years ago. However, as the GC's role steers more to matters of governance it is seen as useful for the GC to be a member. Our own view is that it is not essential for the GC to be a member in the way that the chief people officer really should be a member. Indeed, as far as a full exco goes, it is perhaps safer that the GC remains an adviser (and hopefully a regular attendee) in order that they retain their independence in advising the committee – the angle of independence is much more difficult if you are a member and therefore a decision maker. (This is the reason, too, that the GC and company secretary are very rarely board members.) Given your need to act in the best interests of your client (the organisation) but with a higher regulatory standard rightly imposed upon you, you need to ensure you act independently and objectively at all times in working with the exco.

2.2 Becoming company secretary

It is quite usual for in-house lawyers to become company secretaries too. Indeed, while this might have once been combined with a legal role it is now often a career in its own right for in-house lawyers. For very large corporates, where the role might be too extensive for one person to cover and therefore it might be better to separate out the role of GC/company secretary, the legal and company secretarial team is frequently combined. But that doesn't stop you considering doing some company secretarial work as part of your role or redirecting your career to being a company secretary.

The company secretary is an officer of the company, just as the directors are. While there is no longer a strict requirement for a private company in the United Kingdom to have a company secretary (subject to some exceptions) public limited companies – both listed and unlisted – must have a company secretary. In the main, this person must have certain qualifications – barristers and solicitors are just two who meet the requirements – although the board can widen the scope of their appointment if these particular requirements aren't met. But this isn't a book on the law, as you will probably have noticed! So if you want to find out more about the legal requirements for the role we would recommend looking at *The ICSA Company Secretary's Handbook*, which provides more background.[23] Here we are much more interested in the dynamic and operational aspects of the position of company secretary.

So what do you need to do before you take it on? Most importantly, understand the nature of the role.

One of the best descriptions of the role of the company secretary comes from the Financial Reporting Council's *Guidance on Board Effectiveness*.[24] Indeed, the *Guidance* is a good publication if you want to understand boards generally, their structure and dynamics, and how they work or should work. While the *Guidance* is aimed principally at listed companies, many other companies follow it. Paragraphs 79–85 describe the company secretary's role and include the following:

> *79. The company secretary is responsible for ensuring that board procedures are complied with, advising the board on all governance matters, supporting the chair and helping the board and its committees to function efficiently ...*
>
> *85. The company secretary's effectiveness can be enhanced by building relationships of mutual trust with the chair, the senior independent director and the non-executive directors, while maintaining the confidence of executive director colleagues.* ***They are in a unique position between the executive and the board*** ...[25]

The last point (emphasis ours) is especially important. Having an effective company secretary is an important component of the well-performing board.

One of the biggest challenges with the company secretary role is the need to build good relationships with the most senior people in the company – the directors. And this is more challenging than might at first appear. Often the company secretary will be the only other person in a board meeting with the directors. Yet while the directors are equal to one another, the company secretary is unlikely to be at

One of the biggest challenges with the company secretary role is the need to build good relationships with the most senior people in the company – the directors. And this is more challenging than might at first appear … Good people skills, and the ability to deal with stressful situations, are absolutely essential.

the same level – very few company secretaries are also directors. Good people skills, and the ability to deal with stressful situations, are absolutely essential.

Another challenge – and one that you cannot easily rectify before taking on the role – is that every board tends to see the role of company secretary in a slightly different way.

2.3 Moving away from legal roles

(a) Chief risk officer/head of compliance
These roles often only occur in heavily regulated sectors such as financial services or pharmaceuticals, or where there are major health and safety issues in the sector concerned, such as in construction. However, they provide an option for lawyers to broaden their experience by working in roles often associated with legal ones. It is very common, for example, for in-house lawyers to work alongside heads of compliance or risk and by doing so they will gain an understanding of what these roles entail. Roles like this will, of course, depend on the nature of the organisation and sector concerned but a typical headline job description for a chief risk officer might include the following:

> *The chief risk officer, supported by the risk function, is responsible for ensuring robust, independent oversight and challenge of risk-taking activities across the organisation.*[26]

If you would like to develop your interest in risk or pursue a career in this area, a good guide is the Financial Reporting Council's *Guidance on Risk Management, Internal Control and Related Financial and Business Reporting*.[27]

Compliance roles will have a different remit depending on how a particular organisation complies with the sector's regulatory bodies' rules and regulations. Having a legal background here is of immense benefit as you will have a good understanding already of how regulation works and how it can be best adhered to.

(b) Chief people officer
Although rare, on occasion in-house lawyers develop a career in the human resources department. There are, of course, some transferable skills between legal team and HR. Legal will often be involved in drafting and reviewing company policies, many of which will ultimately sit within HR. Equally, the legal team will often be involved in employment disputes and so should have a good idea of how the HR team works, in which case the fit will be more natural than you might otherwise expect. It perhaps also presents an easier transition to

getting onto the exco or taking up a non-executive role (for more on which, see the next chapter). However, before you embark on trying to secure the role of chief people officer, don't underestimate the scale of the challenge. Despite some people – often lawyers, alas – being sniffy about the HR role, done well (which is not easy) it probably provides more value to the company than any other C-suite role, with the possible exception of CEO. As Heidrick & Struggles' report, *Do you have the right C-Suite?* states:

> *As companies recognize that talent is the most powerful lever for achieving competitive advantage, no role in the C-suite has been transformed more and has delivered more impact on the business than the Chief Human Resources Officer (CHRO). Like the CFO, today's CHRO plays a pivotal role in driving the CEO's agenda. Responsible for what is often the company's biggest investment – its people – the CHRO works at the intersection of strategy and the means to execute it, anticipating where the business is going and making sure that the organization has the talent to take it there. As the CEO's trusted advisor, the CHRO needs to artfully balance this expectation with their role in supporting the board's compensation, nominating and governance committee around total rewards, succession planning and talent risk management.*[28]

Going down this route will provide you with different experience as well as perhaps some new options for the future, towards the end of your executive career.

(c) Head of ethics or sustainability

There are a range of roles within the organisation, different from but allied to legal ones, to which you could transition from in-house lawyer. Two relatively new ones are chief ethics officer and head of sustainability. A chief ethics officer has a similar role to a chief compliance officer and will deal with things such as drafting, approving and implementing codes of ethics, providing training for these and monitoring compliance. Head of sustainability is another, increasingly important role. In 2022 we experienced the joint hottest summer on record;[29] and, of course, such extremes are becoming more common. We only have one world, so we have to look after it. The need to safeguard our planet is something of which companies are only too well aware, and many have taken a proactive approach to ESG (environmental, social and governance) with an emphasis on the 'E'. They have done so largely because they have had to, either through government or customer pressure. Sustainability is now a key focus for many organisations, with the resultant rise of sustainability teams ensuring that companies are doing everything they can to comply with environmental regulations and best practice. So, perhaps another role to think about.

You could, of course, seek a strictly business role – chief of staff, chief operating officer or chief administrative officer – within the organisation, and in the next chapter we will see an example of a lawyer who did just that, with few if any regrets. Going into such roles is not impossible, although it may take a few sideways moves. Once there, your legal training will be an important foundation for your new role, but it is important to remember that if you go into a business role you are no longer part of the legal team, and while it might be tempting to continue to give legal advice to friendly faces within the organisation, you must instead refer them to the in-house legal team.

The final accolade is perhaps to become CEO of an organisation. This is by no means easy, at least in the United Kingdom (easier in the United States). You are far more likely to become CEO with an accounting background (many CFOs go on to become CEO) or if you have previously run a business or division, than if you have been in a support function such as legal or HR. It is not impossible, but making it to CEO – at least of a commercial organisation – in the United Kingdom is rare.

And, finally, you could just leave the law altogether and do something completely different. But that warrants a book in itself!

It is important to think ahead even if you really enjoy your job and believe it will last forever. You may get to a stage ... where even if you don't have to, you still want to change direction and try something new.

VIII. Developing your career after law

This chapter focuses on why you may need to develop a career after law and why you need to plan early. Or is it just luck? The chapter also looks at developing a different style of CV, and why that is a must. Other things to consider:

- Where can you get help?
- Who should you read on the subject?
- Should you become a NED and how do you go about this?

1. The importance of managing your career life

John Cleese, Jerry Springer, Fidel Castro, Henri Matisse and Andrea Bocelli. All very different people – it is kind of hard to imagine Castro performing the parrot sketch – but all with one thing in common: they either were, or started out training to be, lawyers. And all branched out into different careers. Now, we are not suggesting that if you have had a bad day with the CEO you should tell them to stick their job because you are going to retrain as an artist! After all, not everyone is going to be the next Matisse or Banksy; but you should constantly review your career and where it is going, along with your longer-term objectives.
It is important to think ahead even if you really enjoy your job and believe it will last forever. You may get to a stage – as we outline below – where even if you don't have to, you still want to change direction and try something new.

The key thing to remember is that it is important to keep your career under review. Perhaps the first decision is whether you want to maintain your legal role. Many lawyers do and would not dream of doing anything else. For others, the path is less clear-cut. However, even if you do wish to continue, it is prudent to take a sense check from time to time as to how realistic this is. As companies become more reliant on things such as AI, there may be a reduction in the number of employees required, and you may need to re-skill in any case.

2. One reason to develop a post-law career: you may be working at 103!

You might think we are joking, but that is the age of the oldest chair of a listed company (in fact, he is chair of two companies so is clearly pretty busy).[30] And the late Frances Hasselbein, an associate of the late business guru Peter Drucker, was still serving as a NED at over 100! So, if you are coming to the end of your executive career and think the bulk of your working life is over, you might like to think again.

Drucker represents an insightful example to anyone thinking about the next stage of their career and, indeed, life. He started out working in manufacturing, became a journalist, then an economist (picking up a doctorate in international law along the way) and finally a business academic. In his seminal work *Managing Oneself*, he said:

> *At forty-five most executives have reached the peak of their business career and know it. After twenty years of doing very much the same kind of work, they are good at doing their jobs. But few are learning anything anymore ...*[31]

We can argue about actual ages – and *Managing Oneself* was written some time ago, since when the world has changed – but the principle remains the same. Indeed, one of the chairs for whom one of us undertakes board effectiveness reviews has spent nearly as long as a NED as he did as an executive, and he is not yet 70. Do the maths, as they say!

So we wanted to give you a few insights about moving from a legal to a second, parallel career:

Enjoy: As we have outlined above, your second career may last some time – indeed, it may be longer than your executive career. But you will be doing it (hopefully) for different reasons – it is not just about the money. You need to enjoy it! This came home to us when Ian worked with some professionals (accountants rather than lawyers) who were embarking on the second stage of their lives. Not unsurprisingly, they were daunted by it. They asked about the work Ian now does as a consultant and one of them commented, “You obviously really enjoy what you do now.” Ian hadn’t really reflected on this but when he did, he came to realise how true it was. Having spent most of his career as a chief legal officer and company secretary and while (generally) enjoying the work, he was never really happy in corporate life. What he does now is in many ways more challenging (“I work harder and longer than I did as a chief legal officer, and I worked pretty hard at that”) and it is not a certain life, but consulting, coaching, facilitation and training are a fantastic mix. So when moving into the second stage of your career, make sure you find something you enjoy. You are swapping certainty for the unknown – that in itself can be exciting and you need to enjoy it.

Learn: Drucker mentions a number of important points but for us one stands out: learning. “[F]ew are learning anything anymore,”[32] he said in respect of executives. For us, life is about learning, not position or hierarchy. It is perhaps why we don’t miss corporate life. Whatever you decide to do, make sure it is something that will challenge you, stretch your thinking and ensure you discover new things and opportunities. You shouldn’t be doing this (solely) for the money, but because the things you will do are interesting, close to your values and worthwhile. So, choose what you do carefully, but equally, don’t be so cautious that you simply end up repeating what you did in your legal career.

Network: You’ll need to network extensively. Don’t like networking? Get over it! Effective networking is as much as about giving as it is receiving and if you remember that, you shouldn’t go far wrong. It is difficult and challenging at times – we are both introverts, but we have got nearly all our work as consultants through referral, and therefore networking. If you are looking for certain roles then the executive search community will help you, but you would be unwise to rely on this channel alone – you need to create your own if you are to be truly successful in your second career.

Plan ahead: To cite Drucker again (last time – promise!): “There is one requirement for managing the second half of one’s life: to begin creating it long before one enters it.”[33] That is particularly the case when it may be a very long second half. You can never begin this too soon. Many professionals do – they leave it until they have ‘retired’ and find no one knocking at the door. Yes, they were an expert in their executive field and were heavily in demand, but that expertise will not form part of their second career. You need to give this careful thought early on and plan your way forward. Talk to as many people as you can who have been through the process, and be clear on what you want to do. It will take some time and effort and you would be unwise to underestimate that.

3. Or is it just luck?

Of course, moving away from the legal function and a career as a lawyer can have an element of luck about it. We asked Graeme Proudfoot – who became head of investment trusts at Invesco Perpetual and has now embarked on a career as a NED – why he moved into a business role. He had this to say about his journey away from an in-house legal career:

> *It wasn't a conscious decision but I had a good corporate background. I was asked to manage one of the business divisions as well as continuing with my GC role. It took me a long time to decide whether to do one rather than the other – a very difficult decision to go into the business but I have no regrets.*
>
> *To be able to move into the business you do need to have credibility within the businesspeople (other than just being a lawyer). And it will depend upon the nature of the organisation how easy it is to move into a business role. So you need to choose the organisation you join with care – one that wants to stretch you is more likely to give you the right opportunities.*
>
> *You also need to recognise that as an in-house lawyer – even GC – you are not the star of the show. That is the CEO.*

4. Developing a different type of CV

While your career in law can be a great launch pad for a new career – either executive or post-executive – remember that you are transitioning from law. Many of your skills will be transferable but it is important to ensure your CV focuses on those that will be applicable to the type of role you want to move to. We see many lawyers looking to leave in-house legal roles who have produced a great CV, but it is really geared towards getting another in-house legal job. If you are applying to transfer into a new sector, this approach is unlikely to get you very far – beyond a friendly headhunter saying they have this amazing new in-house legal role you might be interested in. The key thing is to identify those of your existing skills and experience that can be transitioned – or can at least be of use – in the new job. Your legal experience will be a useful context but more important will be to identify transferable skills. In addition, of course, you will need to provide some reasoning as to why you want to leave your legal career and what made you interested in the particular job for which you are applying – but these could both perhaps be left for the covering letter.

If you are looking at a post-executive career and going into something such as consultancy, or embarking on a portfolio career with a number of roles such as non-executive directorships, then you need to adapt the format of your CV. (Your CV should always be bespoke to the role for which you are applying, but here we are talking about a more fundamental change in format.) So, for example, if you want to pursue a non-executive portfolio career (not necessarily an easy choice – see below!) then you need to point all of your experience at this. Most senior lawyers will have worked extensively with boards but two of the recent GC who sent us CVs failed to mention this in any great detail – instead, they just recounted their legal experience. Understanding boards and being able to work at board level are key components of being a successful NED, and both these candidates had them in spades but had not bothered to mention them. They should have been in with a really good chance of making the shortlist (or at the very least the longlist) for a NED role, but failed to do so. The trick is to really focus on what will be required in the new roles you are looking at, and identify all relevant experience (and interests) that will whet the appetite of the headhunter. It isn't easy when you are trying to transition, so you need to prepare with care. CVs, when you are moving discipline, should be more thematic, allied to the requirements of the role for which you are applying.

5. Where to get help
Changing direction in your career is a big task and it is sometimes difficult to achieve alone. There are a range of resources for help and

CVs, when you are moving discipline, should be more thematic, allied to the requirements of the role for which you are applying.

Boards now focus on diversity, hopefully in the widest sense of the word, and many people are going on the board as NEDs in their forties, some even in their thirties. Age is a component of diversity too, so don't leave it too late.

advice that you can lean on. First, you can get a mentor, perhaps in your existing workplace and with whom you feel happy to share your plans.

Secondly, there are a number of coaches who specialise in career coaching. We talked about coaching (and mentoring) in some detail in chapter V so we won't dwell on it here. However, particularly with coaching you should ask around about who specialises and is good in this area. Visiting the websites of professional coaching organisations such as the Association for Professional Executive Coaching and Supervision (APECS)[34] or the International Coach Federation[35] may help provide you with some ideas.

Thirdly, you can talk it over with others who have changed careers, to see what they did and what worked for them. How easy did they find it? What wouldn't they do again? Were they able to change careers in one go or did it take more than one move?

Finally, there are a number of books on the subject of changing careers – indeed, far too many to mention here. However, we would recommend two in particular. The first is Peter Drucker's above-mentioned *Managing Oneself* which, although written a little while ago, still has great resonance.[36] And the second is Herminia Ibarra's *Working Identity: Unconventional Strategies for Reinventing Your Career*, a very good guide that suggests you test out different options.[37]

6. Becoming a non-executive director

Finally, we wanted to briefly touch on being a NED, partly because it is a world we know well but also because it is a popular choice for those coming out of an executive career. It is important not to underestimate the scale of the challenge – there are far more candidates than there are (paid) roles. If you have a professional skill, that will be useful but will only take you so far. Lawyers often complain that it is difficult for them to get NED roles (it is!), claiming their skills must be useful for the role. What they are forgetting is that they are not being hired principally for their professional skills but more for their commercial ones, or their knowledge of a particular sector. So if you are a lawyer or accountant who specialised in property you might be attractive to a property company. But you must bring something more to the party than just your profession. And an earlier point is also relevant: boards now focus on diversity, hopefully in the widest sense of the word, and many people are going on the board as NEDs in their forties, some even in their thirties. Age is a component of diversity too, so don't leave it too late.

If you want to go down the route of becoming a NED, here are a few tips:

- As outlined above, don't leave it too late in your career. And never, ever look at it as a retirement job! Boards don't want a bunch of retired and tired executives sitting around the boardroom table – the role is too important for that. As we have already said, people are now going on boards much earlier, so starting a NED career in your sixties is unlikely to work. If you can combine a NED role with your executive career then that will be good for you, your existing company and the one that you will join as a NED. But remember, as a director, you are responsible ultimately for all that the company does and so, if there is a crisis, you may have to put your NED role before that of your executive one – make sure you can do this!
- Don't underestimate the time commitment. If it says the role is 36 days a year you can double or triple that if there is a crisis or any type of M&A activity. And as mentioned above, you will have to put your NED role first in these circumstances. You should also bear in mind that you are more likely to have to give a greater time commitment in the first year or so on the board, getting up to speed with the company.
- Create a wining NED CV (see above)!
- Get a good headhunter behind you who will support your cause and advocate for you. Do some research on the best ones that specialise in NED roles and try to speak with them. A very good website to look at for NED roles is Nurole, which contains both details on roles and lots of guidance on becoming a NED.[38]
- Read up as much as you can on boards and corporate governance generally. If you are a corporate lawyer this may be an area you know well, but if not it is important to have a good understanding of how (effective) boards work and operate. There are a number of corporate governance codes that you should look at – the 2018 *UK Corporate Governance Code*,[39] published by the Financial Reporting Council, and the FRC's *Guidance on Board Effectiveness* from the same year,[40] are good places to start. But there are other good books on boards generally.
- There are a number of effective and short training courses on being a NED, run by organisations such as Cranfield School of Management, which should give you a solid foundation for understanding what the role entails.[41]
- Finally, speak to your existing board members if you can, or others who have taken on NED roles. What has their experience been like? Have they enjoyed the role? What are their tips on securing a NED role (it is always the first one that is the most difficult to secure)? Once you have that, then it is easier to get further roles, but don't become a serial NED!

IX. Some final words of wisdom

1. Advice and tips

We thought it would be helpful to conclude this Special Report with some words of advice and useful tips from lawyers who have taken the leap to move from practice to in-house.

Paul Freeman, senior legal counsel and head of enforcement, Isle of Man Financial Services Authority

Why did you become a lawyer?

I enjoyed analysing problems. It was a gradual process. But it played to my skills.

Why did you choose to move in-house?

I thought about it a lot earlier in my career but it never quite worked out the way I wanted it to. I became an aviation lawyer (and a pilot in my spare time!) because I was interested in the sector but I couldn't get the right role in-house in this sector. However, I kept my eye on going in-house and looked for opportunities.

What stage of a private practice lawyer's career is the best time to go in-house? Is there an ideal time?

It really comes down to personal choice. Do you like business development and winning work? If so, you might prefer to build a career in private practice. However, whatever you decide I think you need five to six years PQE before making the transition. By this time you should have enough experience to stand your ground – you'll have the requisite degree of confidence. However, if you leave it too late you may become pigeonholed and find it difficult to go in-house. I went from being a law firm partner to a GC role so it is possible to go in-house later on in your career.

What are your tips for moving in-house?

- You'll need to be more of a generalist as you will deal with a much wider range of issues.
- You need to be very pragmatic – be able to cut to the chase on advice.
- Businesspeople don't want reams of legal advice – they just want an answer and the options.
- Bear in mind that it can be lonelier in-house as you don't have the same degree of support.

How different is it from being in private practice?
You need to be more attuned to the business but then you don't have to go out and sell!

Can you go back? Would you?
While I miss some of the aspects of my aviation and insurance work that I undertook in private practice, I am glad I made the move and would prefer to stay in-house.

Does it give you other career options?
Yes, both during your in-house career and after. So you can go and work in the business in a non-legal role and had I gone in-house earlier I would like to have done so.

How much more of a businessperson do you need to be?
Much more so – focus on strategy, risk; be more generalist.

Brian Littleton, head of in-house legal recruitment, Chadwick Nott

What stage of a private practice lawyer's career is the best time to go in-house? Is there an ideal time?
The ideal time is mid-level – three to five years PQE. You will have a greater number of opportunities at this stage – the more senior you become, the top of the pyramid is smaller unless you are prepared to go in at a lower level. However, it is not impossible after this stage. While it is possible to go in at partner level this is easier if you are known to the board of the company you are joining or you are an M&A lawyer.

The most appropriate background is general corporate/commercial and IT. Other specialisms may be more cyclical or not have a broad enough appeal.

What are your tips for moving in-house?

- Look at as many opportunities as possible.
- Go for lots of interviews even if you don't initially think you'll like the role – you may be surprised the further you get down the process. And, of course, it is good practice.
- Talk to others who are already in-house.
- Be down to earth – businesses are generally more like this than professional services firms.
- When you are in-house don't act like a Magic Circle firm partner!
- You'll do less technical law in-house so you need to ensure this is for you.
- It is much faster moving than private practice – generally.
- Doing a few secondments beforehand will give you an idea whether it is for you.
- Don't think it will be an easier workload – generally it won't be!

How different is it from being in private practice?
There is less business development! If you enjoy BD and are good at it maybe you are better off in private practice.

Can you go back?
You can but it is rare. You won't have a following unless you can bring your former employer as an anchor client.

Does it give you other career options?
Yes, especially in US banks and financial services organisations. Moving into commercial roles is easier at both US banks and US companies. The lawyer's training and skill set is simply viewed as more transferable and there is generally a strong history of ex-lawyers thriving in commercial roles in US banks and US companies.

Graeme Proudfoot, non-executive director and chairman

Why did you become a lawyer?
I enjoyed watching *Crown Court* and *Rumpole* and that inspired me. I also got some legal experience before university working for the British Shipbuilders' in-house legal department, and that spurred my interest too.

Why did you choose to move in-house?
I had some previous experience of in-house in my gap year and while I enjoyed my time in private practice, the firm I was working

for was changing and so I looked for in-house opportunities. I didn't pursue any private practice opportunities.

What stage of a private practice lawyer's career is the best time to go in-house? Is there an ideal time?
It is better to do it earlier than later because you will probably be more flexible in your approach and that makes it easier to adapt to the style of the company you are joining. This will vary considerably, whereas law firms tend to have a similar style.

What are your tips for moving in-house?

- I liked the idea of being a senior partner in a law firm but had little appetite for the route to get there. I am keen on relationship and people management and it is useful to remember that you often get the chance to focus on these earlier on in-house than you would do in private practice.
- The flip side is that you have less power and perhaps less influence in-house. You can lay down the law more as a private practice lawyer with your clients – it is more difficult to do this in-house and you need to use influence subtly rather than being dogmatic.
- You need to recognise that as an in-house lawyer – even as a GC – you are not the star of the show. That is the CEO.

You moved into a business role. Why was that?
It wasn't a conscious decision but I had a good corporate background. I was asked to manage one of the business divisions as well as continuing with my GC role. It took me a long time to decide whether to do one rather than the other – it was a very difficult decision to go into the business but I have no regrets.

To be able to move into the business you do need to have credibility with the business people (other than just being a lawyer); and it will depend upon the nature of the organisation how easy it is to move into a business role. So you need to choose the organisation you join with care – one that wants to stretch you is more likely to give you the right opportunities.

Katy Ruddell, senior counsel, Farrer & Co

Why did you become a lawyer?
I thought it would provide me with lots of opportunities.

Why did you choose to move in-house?
When I was training I went on secondment to an asset management company and really liked the environment. The variety appealed to me and I really enjoyed seeing projects from start to finish, which is something you often don't get in private practice.

What stage of a private practice lawyer's career is the best time to go in-house? Is there an ideal time?
Two to three years PQE.

What are your tips for moving in-house?
You need to be both flexible and robust: flexible because you will have to deal with a range of work but robust because you need to have the confidence to stand up to the business on occasion and provide them with advice that they might not always like. You also need to be creative in your approach.

How different is it from being in private practice?
As I have said, an in-house role will give you the opportunity to see a project from start to finish. However, there is less technical law and you will often act more as a project manager than a lawyer.

And why did you go back? Which is best?
I wanted to resume my career after having a career break. It is now much easier to traverse between private practice and in-house (both ways). The advantage of now being in private practice but having been in-house is that you appreciate that advice for clients needs to be practical: you understand more about the recipient of advice and their need for succinct guidance. I have enjoyed both private practice and in-house – both have pros and cons. I am enjoying doing more law now and solving problems. Equally, in-house is probably now much busier [stressful] than it once was.

An interview with an in-house lawyer (anonymous)

Why did you become a lawyer?
At school I either wanted to be a lawyer or a doctor but my A-level choices pushed me more towards law. While I had no burning desire to change the world, I did want to have a profession and the academic challenge of law appealed.

Why did you choose to move in-house?
My career route has been a bit different to a 'standard' legal one. I started as an in-house lawyer in Europe (having completed an English law degree and then the English LPC, part-time (and mostly remotely) for two years whilst working in Europe) and came back to the UK to qualify here. I trained with a well-known London law firm and qualified as a corporate lawyer.

Working in private practice allowed me to develop my technical legal skills. While I loved working as a corporate lawyer – I am an adrenaline junkie and love M&A deals – I was working every hour and knew I had to get more of a work–life balance (but see what I say below!).

What stage of a private practice lawyer's career is the best time to go in-house? Is there an ideal time?
Well every situation is different, of course, but a good time is when you are between five and seven years PQE. I do think you need to develop your technical legal skills and you'll do that better in private practice where there is generally more support and resource around. While you can go in later it may be more difficult to adapt – in-house is very different. Still, some people manage to go in-house at partner stage but they are normally going in as the GC.

What are your tips for moving in-house?

- Despite what I have said above, don't expect it necessarily to give you a better work–life balance. I still work very long hours!
- Don't have set expectations and keep an open mind. In-house is not normally as well structured as private practice. There is less support – few PAs, templates, support lawyers so Practical Law will soon become your best friend![42]
- You need to enjoy being part of the business so it is best to choose a sector you'll enjoy and are interested in if you can. That was one of my main objectives.
- And this means working more with non-lawyers which can, of course, be a bonus!
- It will take time to get to know the business and the sector.

Can you go back? Would you?
Yes, I think you can and I wouldn't rule it out.

Does it give you other career options?
Yes, lots of lawyers decide to go into the business.

How much more of a businessperson do you need to be?
More so than in private practice. You need to know the business well because often you will be the decision maker (despite what others tell you!).

2. Concluding thoughts

To conclude this Special Report, here are some words of advice as you go about developing as an in-house lawyer.

- It will largely be up to you to plan and organise your development – you may not have the support of a large HR/L&D function or a large in-house legal team. Therefore, you will need to find a way to self-motivate to take the steps and put in the time to do self-development.
- Also look for a range of sources of help – both colleagues in the business and in-house lawyers in other organisations who can act as mentors, and also professional business coaches.

- Find out what fires up and enthuses other people in your business to develop and progress.
- Remember that development should not only, or mainly, be about correcting weaknesses. Therefore, notice what you are good at and seek feedback from others. They may be more aware than you about what you do really well. Look to build on those strengths and find new situations where you can put them to good use.
- Always seek to develop the whole you, not just the legal/business you.

Good luck!

Endnotes

1 Ian White and Simon McCall, *Your Role as General Counsel: How to Survive and Thrive in your Role as GC*, Globe Law and Business, 2021.
2 Peter F Drucker, *Management Challenges for the 21st Century*, PerfectBound, 1999, p163.
3 Paul Gilbert, "The seventy-five year career", LBC Wise Counsel blog, 19 June 2022. Available at: www.lbcwisecounsel.com/resources/articles/article/the-seventy-five-year-career/#.Y_NntC-l1z8.
4 Drucker, *Management Challenges for the 21st Century*, *supra* note 2.
5 See Peter Drucker, *The Five Most Important Questions You Will Ever Ask About Your Organisation*, Jossey-Bass, 2008; and Charles Handy, *Understanding Organisations*, 4th edn, Penguin, 1993.
6 A searchable directory of MBA programmes is available on the AMBA website at: www.associationofmbas.com/school-search/.
7 White and McCall, *Your Role as General Counsel*, *supra* note 1.
8 Daniel H Pink, *Drive: The Surprising Truth About What Motivates Us*, Canongate Books, 2011.
9 The remark was made in the context of the MBA in Legal Practice programme on which Simon McCall was a tutor from 1993 to 2003.
10 White and McCall, *Your Role as General Counsel*, *supra* note 1.
11 David H Maister, Charles H Green and Robert M Galford, *The Trusted Advisor: 20th Anniversary Edition*, Free Press, 2021.
12 The question was put by a managing partner during a discussion group on a residential programme for law firm managing partners run by Nottingham Law School (where Simon McCall was part of the programme faculty).
13 This handbook was created by the coaches (among them Simon McCall) in Sherwood PSF Consulting to act as a guide for people (particularly in law firms) who wanted to find out more about coaching and how it could help lawyers at all levels.
14 See chapter II above, "Moving in-house"; see also "The first 100 days", in Ian White and Simon McCall, *Your Role as General Counsel*, *supra* note 1.
15 See Tim Gallwey, *The Inner Game of Tennis* (Pan, 2015) and other *Inner Game* titles; and Myles Downey, who was influenced by the work of Tim Gallwey and led Simon McCall's coaching training programme at The School of Coaching in 2004. Downey is the author of *Effective Modern Coaching – the principles and art of successful business coaching*, LID Publishing, 2014.
16 Bob Bates, *The Little Book of Big Coaching Models: 76 ways to help managers get the best out of people*, Pearson, 2015.
17 Nancy Kline, *The Ten Components of a Thinking Environment*. Available at: www.timetothink.com/thinking-environment/the-ten-components/.
18 Available at: www.neilswheel.org.
19 "Mentoring and Career Development with Paul Gilbert", *LBC Wise Counsel website*. Available at: www.lbcwisecounsel.com/lawyer-mentoring/#.Y_ODly-l1z8.
20 *Ibid.*
21 White and McCall, *Your Role as General Counsel*, *supra* note 1.
22 Heidrick & Struggles, *Do you have the right C-Suite? Tough questions CEOs today are asking*, 2013. Available at: www.yumpu.com/en/document/read/43192305/do-you-have-the-right-c-suite-heidrick-struggles.
23 Douglas Armour, *The ICSA Company Secretary's Handbook*, 11th edn, ICSA Publishing Ltd, 2016.
24 Financial Reporting Council, *Guidance on Board Effectiveness*, July 2018. Available at: www.frc.org.uk/getattachment/61232f60-a338-471b-ba5a-bfed25219147/2018-guidance-on-board-effectiveness-final.pdf.
25 *Ibid*, paras 79–85.
26 The Risk Coalition, *Guidance: Raising the Bar*, 2019. Available at: www.riskcoalition.org.uk/the-guidance.
27 Financial Reporting Council, *Guidance on Risk Management, Internal Control and Related Financial and Business Reporting*, September 2014. Available at: www.frc.org.uk/getattachment/d672c107-b1fb-4051-84b0-f5b83a1b93f6/Guidance-on-Risk-Management-Internal-Control-and-Related-Reporting.pdf.
28 Heidrick & Struggles, *Do you have the right C-Suite?*, *supra* note 22.
29 Met Office, "Joint hottest summer on record for England", Press Office, 1 September 2022. Available at: www.metoffice.gov.uk/about-us/press-office/news/weather-and-climate/2022/joint-hottest-summer-on-record-for-england.
30 Jacques Gaston Murray, chair of Andrew Sykes plc and London Security plc.
31 Peter F Drucker, *Managing Oneself*, Harvard Business Review Press, 2008, p185.
32 *Ibid*, p189.
33 *Ibid*, p192.
34 See: www.apecs.org/.
35 See: https://coachingfederation.org/.
36 Drucker, *Managing Oneself*, *supra* note 31.
37 Herminia Ibarra, *Working Identity: Unconventional Strategies for Reinventing Your Career*, Harvard Business Review Press, 2004.
38 See: www.nurole.com.
39 Available at: www.frc.org.uk/getattachment/88bd8c45-50ea-4841-95b0-d2f4f48069a2/2018-UK-Corporate-Governance-Code-FINAL.pdf.

40 Available at: www.frc.org.uk/getattachment/61232f60-a338-471b-ba5a-bfed25219147/2018-guidance-on-board-effectiveness-final.pdf.
41 For example, Cranfield's Non-Executive Directors' Seminar in April 2023.
42 Thomson Reuters' Practical Law, the online legal know-how resource, is available at: https://uk.practicallaw.thomsonreuters.com/Browse/Home/About/AboutUs?navId=33BFCFAA103D185F1208FC6C019D5F75&comp=pluk&transitionType=Default&contextData=%28sc.Default%29.

About the authors

Ian White
Board effectiveness consultant and coach
Programme leader, Cranfield Non-executive Director programme
ian.white@ianrobertwhite.co.uk

Ian White is a former chief legal officer and company secretary for both listed and private companies. While he has spent most of his career as a lawyer, he also has an MBA and has spent some time working as a strategy consultant.

Ian now works as a consultant, coach, trainer and facilitator. His previous in-house experience has led him to develop expertise in corporate governance, working with boards, leaders and lawyers on effectiveness, enhancement and performance. He spends much of his time reviewing and advising boards and management teams on structure, dynamics and how they can excel in leading their organisations. While his main focus is on FTSE 100/250 and major private companies, he also works with professional services firms, public sector bodies and a number of charities and other not-for-profit organisations.

Ian also helps lawyers, both in-house and in private practice, to work more closely and effectively with their clients, encouraging them to think of themselves as businesspeople first and lawyers second.

Simon McCall
Director, Sherwood PSF Consulting Limited
simon.mccall@sherwoodpsfconsulting.com

Simon McCall is a management consultant and business coach. He works mainly with lawyers, in private practice and in-house. Over 30 years, his consulting assignments have included helping in-house departments to develop a compelling strategy and law firm management teams to work more effectively together. Simon has designed and led management development programmes for lawyers at associate and partner level. As a coach, Simon has enabled lawyers to explore and plan changes to how they work and how they build successful relationships with colleagues.

Simon has a law degree from the University of Cambridge and qualified as a solicitor in 1980 with Lawrence Graham. He then worked in-house with Houlder Offshore (an oil drilling business) and American Express. He has an MBA from the Cranfield School of Management. Simon was a principal tutor on the Nottingham Law School MBA in legal practice and did his coaching training with The School of Coaching.

About Globe Law and Business

Globe Law and Business was established in 2005. From the very beginning, we set out to create law books that are sufficiently high level to be of real use to the experienced professional, yet still accessible and easy to navigate. Most of our authors are drawn from Magic Circle and other top commercial firms, both in the United Kingdom and internationally.

Our titles are carefully produced, with the utmost attention paid to editorial, design and production processes. We hope this results in high-quality publications that are easy to read and a pleasure to own. Our titles are also available as ebooks, which are compatible with most desktop, laptop and tablet devices. In 2018 we expanded our portfolio to include journals and Special Reports, available both digitally and in hard copy format, and produced to the same high standards as our books.

In 2021, we were very pleased to announce the start of a new chapter for Globe Law and Business following the acquisition of law books under the imprint Ark Publishing. Our law firm management list is now significantly expanded with many well known and loved Ark Publishing titles.

We are also pleased to announce the launch of our online content platform, Globe Law Online. This allows for easy search and networked access across firms. Key collections include the Law Firm Management Collection, Private Client and Energy and the Energy Transition. Email me at sian@globelawandbusiness.com for further details or to arrange a free trial for you or your firm.

Sian O'Neill
Managing director
Globe Law and Business
www.globelawandbusiness.com

Notes and ideas